BBQ
Made Easy

The Basics

Nothing is more mouthwatering than the smoky aroma of juicy burgers barbecuing outside on a blue-sky summer day... or more satisfying than cutting into a perfectly grilled steak on a starlit night. And for those of you who think that only master chefs can create these melt-in-your-mouth masterpieces, *BBQ Made Easy* is here to prove you wrong.

By reviewing the following basics and easy step-by-step recipes, you will soon be grilling like the pros!

BASIC FIRE

• Always place the grill on a solid surface, set away from shrubbery, grass and overhangs.

• NEVER use alcohol, gasoline or kerosene as a lighter fluid starter—all three can cause an explosion.

• To get a sluggish fire going, place two or three additional coals in a small metal can and add lighter fluid. Then, stack them on the coals in the grill and light with a match.

• Keep a water-filled spray bottle near the grill to quench flare-ups.

• Remember: hot coals create a hot grill, grid, tools and food. Always wear heavy-duty fireproof mitts to protect your hands.

• The number of coals required for barbecuing depends on the size and type of grill and the amount of food to be prepared. As a general rule, it takes about 30 coals to grill one pound of meat.

• To light a charcoal fire, arrange the coals in a pyramid shape 20 to 30 minutes prior to cooking. The pyramid shape provides enough ventilation for the coals to catch. To start with lighter fluid, soak the coals with about ½ cup lighter fluid. Wait one minute to allow the fluid to soak into the coals and light with a match.

• To light a charcoal fire using a chimney starter, remove the grid from the grill and place the chimney starter in the base of the grill. Crumble a few sheets of newspaper and place them in the bottom portion of the chimney starter. Fill the top portion with coals. Light the newspaper. The coals should be ready in about 20 to 30 minutes.

• The coals are ready when they are about 80% ash gray during daylight and glowing at night.

• To lower the cooking temperature, spread the coals farther apart or raise the grid. To raise the cooking temperature, either lower the grid or move the coals closer together and tap off the ash.

CHECKING CHARCOAL TEMPERATURE

A quick, easy way to estimate the temperature of the coals is to hold your hand, palm side down, about 4 inches above the coals. Count the number of seconds you can hold your hand in that position before the heat forces you to pull it away.

Seconds	Coal Temperature
2	hot, 375°F or more
3	medium-hot, 350° to 375°F
4	medium, 300° to 350°F
5	low, 200° to 300°F

BASIC COOKING METHODS

Direct Cooking

The food is placed on the grid directly over the coals. Make sure there is enough charcoal in a single layer to extend 1 or 2 inches beyond the area of the food on the grill. This method is for quick-cooking foods, such as steaks, chops, hamburgers, kabobs and fish.

Indirect Cooking

The food is placed on the grid over a metal or disposable foil drip pan with the coals banked either to one side or on both sides of the pan. This method is for slow, even cooking of foods, such as large cuts of meat and whole chickens.

When barbecuing by indirect cooking for more than 45 minutes, extra briquets will need to be added to maintain a constant temperature.

Drugstore Wrap

Place the food in the center of an oblong piece of heavy-duty foil, leaving at least a two-inch border around the food. Bring the two long sides together above the food; fold down in a series of locked folds, allowing for heat circulation and expansion.

Fold the short ends up and over again. Press folds firmly to seal the foil packet.

BASIC TIPS

• Always use tongs or a spatula when handling meat. Avoid piercing the meat with a fork.

• Always serve cooked food from the grill on a *clean* plate, not one that held the raw food.

• The cooking rack, or grid, should be kept clean and free from any bits of charred food. Scrub the grid with a stiff brush while it is still warm.

• Watch foods carefully during grilling. Total cooking time will vary with the type of food, position on the grill, weather, temperature of the coals and the degree of doneness you desire. Set a timer to remind you when it's time to check the food on the grill.

• Store charcoal in a dry place. Charcoal won't burn well if it is damp.

• Top and bottom vents should be open before starting a charcoal grill. Close vents when cooking is finished to extinguish the coals.

• The best way to judge the doneness of meat is with a high-quality meat thermometer. Prior to grilling, insert the thermometer into the center of the largest muscle of the meat with the point away from bone or fat. An instant-read thermometer gives an accurate reading within seconds of insertion, although it is not heatproof and should not be left in the meat during grilling.

BASIC TEMPERATURES

This chart gives the basic internal temperatures of meat to determine cooking doneness.

	Doneness	Temperature
Poultry		180°F (170°F in the breast)
Pork		160°F
Beef	Rare	140°F
	Medium-rare	150°F
	Medium	160°F
	Well done	170°F
Lamb		160°F

Grilled Flank Steak with Horseradish Sauce

1 pound beef flank steak
2 tablespoons soy sauce
1 tablespoon red wine
  vinegar
2 cloves garlic, minced
½ teaspoon black pepper

Horseradish Sauce
  (recipe follows)
6 sourdough rolls, split
6 romaine lettuce leaves
  Small pickles (optional)

PLACE steak in large resealable plastic food storage bag. Add soy sauce, vinegar, garlic and pepper. Close bag securely, turning to coat. Marinate in refrigerator at least 1 hour.

PREPARE grill for direct cooking. Drain steak; discard marinade. Place steak on grid. Grill over medium-high heat 5 minutes. Turn steak; grill 6 minutes for medium-rare or until desired doneness. Remove steak from grill. Cover with foil; let stand 15 minutes. Thinly slice steak across grain.

PREPARE Horseradish Sauce. Spread rolls with sauce; layer with sliced steak and lettuce. Garnish with small pickles, if desired.

Makes 6 servings

Horseradish Sauce

1 cup sour cream
1 tablespoon prepared
  horseradish
1 tablespoon Dijon mustard

¼ cup finely chopped fresh
  parsley
½ teaspoon salt

COMBINE all ingredients in small bowl until well blended.

Makes about 1¼ cups

GUEST CH

CHECK NUMBER	SERVER	TABLE
4948	3	4

Seafood Kabobs

1 pound raw large shrimp, peeled and deveined
10 ounces skinless swordfish or halibut steaks, cut into 1-inch cubes

2 tablespoons honey mustard
2 teaspoons fresh lemon juice
8 slices bacon
Lemon wedges and fresh herbs (optional)

SPRAY grid with nonstick cooking spray. Prepare grill for direct cooking.

PLACE shrimp and swordfish in shallow glass dish. Combine mustard and lemon juice in small bowl. Pour over shrimp mixture; toss lightly to coat.

PIERCE one 12-inch metal skewer through 1 end of bacon slice. Add 1 piece shrimp. Pierce skewer through bacon slice again, wrapping bacon slice around 1 side of shrimp. Add 1 piece swordfish. Pierce bacon slice again, wrapping bacon around opposite side of swordfish. Continue adding seafood and wrapping with bacon, pushing ingredients to middle of skewer until end of bacon slice is reached. Repeat with 7 more skewers. Brush any remaining mustard mixture over skewers.

PLACE skewers on grid. Grill, covered, over medium heat 8 to 10 minutes or until shrimp are opaque and swordfish flakes easily when tested with fork, turning halfway through grilling time. Garnish with lemon wedges and fresh herbs, if desired.

Makes 4 servings

Cook's Nook

Kabobs can be prepared up to 3 hours before grilling. Cover and refrigerate until ready to grill.

Mexicali Burgers

1 pound ground beef
⅓ cup salsa or picante
    sauce
⅓ cup crushed tortilla chips
3 tablespoons finely
    chopped fresh cilantro
2 tablespoons grated onion

1 teaspoon ground cumin
4 slices Monterey Jack or
    Cheddar cheese
4 kaiser rolls or hamburger
    buns, split
½ cup purchased or favorite
    recipe guacamole

PREPARE grill for indirect cooking.

COMBINE beef, salsa, tortilla chips, cilantro, onion and cumin in medium bowl. Mix lightly, but thoroughly. Shape mixture into four ½-inch-thick burgers.

PLACE burgers on grid directly over drip pan. Grill, covered, over medium heat 8 to 10 minutes for medium or until desired doneness, turning halfway through grilling time.

PLACE 1 slice cheese on each burger to melt during last 1 to 2 minutes of grilling. If desired, place rolls, cut side down, on grid to toast lightly during last 1 to 2 minutes of grilling. Remove burgers and rolls from grill. Place burgers between rolls; top cheese with guacamole.

Makes 4 servings

Serving Suggestion: Serve with tortilla chips, lettuce and tomato.

Cook's Nook

If making your own guacamole, be sure to use avocados that are somewhat overripe. Cover the guacamole with plastic wrap directly on the surface of the dip to reduce browning and always keep it refrigerated.

Maple Francheezies

Mustard Spread (recipe
  follows)
¼ cup maple syrup
2 teaspoons garlic powder
1 teaspoon black pepper
½ teaspoon ground nutmeg

4 slices bacon
4 jumbo hot dogs
4 hot dog buns, split
½ cup (2 ounces) shredded
  Cheddar cheese

PREPARE Mustard Spread; set aside.

PREPARE grill for direct cooking.

COMBINE maple syrup, garlic powder, pepper and nutmeg in small bowl. Brush syrup mixture onto bacon slices. Wrap 1 slice bacon around each hot dog.

BRUSH hot dogs with remaining syrup mixture. Place hot dogs on grid. Grill, covered, over medium-high heat 8 minutes or until bacon is crisp and hot dogs are heated through, turning halfway through grilling time. Spread buns with Mustard Spread. Place hot dogs in buns; top evenly with cheese.   *Makes 4 servings*

Mustard Spread

½ cup prepared yellow
  mustard
1 tablespoon finely
  chopped onion
1 tablespoon diced tomato

1 tablespoon chopped
  fresh parsley
1 teaspoon garlic powder
½ teaspoon black pepper

COMBINE all ingredients in small bowl; mix well.

Makes about ¾ cup

Serving Suggestion: Serve with potato chips and carrot sticks.

Grilled Pork and Potatoes Vesuvio

1 center-cut boneless pork
loin roast (1½ pounds),
well trimmed and cut
into 1-inch cubes
½ cup dry white wine
2 tablespoons olive oil
4 cloves garlic, minced and
divided

1½ to 2 pounds small red
potatoes, scrubbed
6 lemon wedges
Salt (optional)
Black pepper (optional)
¼ cup chopped fresh
parsley
1 teaspoon finely grated
lemon peel

PLACE pork in large resealable plastic food storage bag. Combine wine, oil and 3 cloves minced garlic in small bowl; pour over pork.

PLACE potatoes in single layer in microwavable dish. Pierce each potato with tip of sharp knife. Microwave at HIGH 6 to 7 minutes or until almost tender when pierced with fork. (Or, place potatoes in large saucepan. Cover with cold water. Bring to a boil over high heat. Simmer 12 minutes or until almost tender when pierced with fork.) Immediately rinse with cold water; drain. Add to bag with pork. Close bag securely, turning to coat. Marinate in refrigerator at least 2 hours or up to 8 hours, turning occasionally.

PREPARE grill for direct cooking.

DRAIN pork mixture; discard marinade. Alternately thread about 3 pork cubes and 2 potatoes onto each of six 12-inch metal skewers. Place 1 lemon wedge on end of each skewer. Sprinkle salt and pepper over pork and potatoes, if desired.

PLACE skewers on grid. Grill, covered, over medium heat 14 to 16 minutes or until pork is juicy and barely pink in center and potatoes are tender, turning halfway through grilling time.

REMOVE skewers from grill. Combine parsley, lemon peel and remaining 1 clove minced garlic in small bowl. Sprinkle over pork and potatoes. Squeeze lemon wedges over pork and potatoes. Garnish as desired.   *Makes 6 servings*

Serving Suggestion: Serve with grilled croutons.

The All-American Burger

¼ cup Burger Spread
  (recipe follows)
1½ pounds ground beef
  2 tablespoons chopped
    fresh parsley
  2 teaspoons onion powder
  2 teaspoons Worcestershire
    sauce

1 teaspoon garlic powder
1 teaspoon black pepper
  Lettuce leaves (optional)
4 hamburger buns, split
  Apple slices (optional)

PREPARE Burger Spread; set aside.

PREPARE grill for direct cooking.

COMBINE beef, parsley, onion powder, Worcestershire sauce, garlic powder and pepper in medium bowl; mix lightly, but thoroughly. Shape mixture into four ½-inch-thick burgers.

PLACE burgers on grid. Grill, covered, over medium heat 8 to 10 minutes for medium or until desired doneness, turning halfway through grilling time.

REMOVE burgers from grill. Place burgers and lettuce leaves, if desired, between buns; top each burger with 1 tablespoon Burger Spread. Garnish with apple slices, if desired.   *Makes 4 servings*

Burger Spread

½ cup ketchup
¼ cup prepared mustard
2 tablespoons chopped
  onion

1 tablespoon relish *or*
  chopped pickles
1 tablespoon chopped
  fresh parsley

COMBINE all ingredients in small bowl; mix well.   *Makes 1 cup*

Marinated Italian Sausage and Peppers

½ cup olive oil
¼ cup red wine vinegar
2 tablespoons chopped
  fresh parsley
1 tablespoon dried oregano
  leaves
2 cloves garlic, crushed
1 teaspoon salt
1 teaspoon black pepper

4 hot or sweet Italian
  sausage links
1 large red onion, sliced
  into rings
1 large bell pepper, sliced
  into wedges
Horseradish-Mustard
  Spread (recipe follows)

COMBINE oil, vinegar, parsley, oregano, garlic, salt and black pepper in small bowl. Place sausages, onion and bell pepper in large resealable plastic food storage bag; pour oil mixture into bag. Close bag securely, turning to coat. Marinate in refrigerator 1 to 2 hours.

PREPARE Horseradish-Mustard Spread; cover and refrigerate until serving time.

PREPARE grill for direct cooking. Drain sausages, onion and bell pepper; reserve marinade.

PLACE sausages on grid. Grill, covered, over high heat 4 to 5 minutes. Turn sausages and place onion and bell pepper on grid. Brush sausages and vegetables with reserved marinade. Grill, covered, 5 minutes or until vegetables are crisp-tender, turning vegetables halfway through grilling time.

SERVE sausages, onion and bell pepper with Horseradish-Mustard Spread.   *Makes 4 servings*

Horseradish-Mustard Spread

3 tablespoons mayonnaise
1 tablespoon prepared
  horseradish
1 tablespoon Dijon mustard

1 tablespoon chopped
  fresh parsley
2 teaspoons garlic powder
1 teaspoon black pepper

COMBINE all ingredients in small bowl; mix well.
                                         Makes about ½ cup

Curried Walnut Grain Burgers

2 eggs
⅓ cup plain yogurt
2 teaspoons
    Worcestershire sauce
2 teaspoons curry powder
½ teaspoon salt
¼ teaspoon ground red
    pepper
1⅓ cups cooked couscous or
    brown rice
½ cup finely chopped
    walnuts

½ cup grated carrot
½ cup minced green onions
⅓ cup fine, dry plain bread
    crumbs
4 sesame seed hamburger
    buns, split
Honey mustard
Thinly sliced cucumber or
    apple
Carrot sticks and fresh
    sprouts (optional)

COMBINE eggs, yogurt, Worcestershire sauce, curry powder, salt and pepper in large bowl; beat until blended. Stir in couscous, walnuts, carrot, green onions and bread crumbs. Shape into four 1-inch-thick burgers.

SPRAY grid with nonstick cooking spray. Prepare grill for direct cooking.

PLACE burgers on grid. Grill, covered, over medium-high heat 10 to 12 minutes, turning halfway through grilling time. Serve on buns with mustard and cucumber. Garnish with carrot sticks and sprouts, if desired.

Makes 4 servings

Chicken Teriyaki

· ·

8 large chicken drumsticks
    (about 2 pounds)
⅓ cup prepared teriyaki
    sauce
2 tablespoons brandy or
    apple juice
1 green onion, minced

1 tablespoon vegetable oil
1 teaspoon ground ginger
½ teaspoon sugar
¼ teaspoon garlic powder
    Prepared sweet and sour
    sauce (optional)

PLACE chicken in large resealable plastic food storage bag. Combine teriyaki sauce, brandy, onion, oil, ginger, sugar and garlic powder in small bowl; pour over chicken. Close bag securely, turning to coat. Marinate in refrigerator at least 1 hour or overnight, turning occasionally.

PREPARE grill for indirect cooking.

DRAIN chicken; reserve marinade. Place chicken on grid directly over drip pan. Grill, covered, over medium heat 45 minutes or until chicken is no longer pink in center and juices run clear, turning and brushing with reserved marinade every 15 minutes. Discard remaining marinade. Serve with sweet and sour sauce, if desired.

Makes 4 servings

Serving Suggestion: Serve with potato salad and fresh melon wedges.

Southwestern Lamb Chops with Charred Corn Relish

....

4 lamb shoulder or blade chops (about 8 ounces each), cut ¾ inch thick	1 teaspoon ground cumin
¼ cup vegetable oil	¼ teaspoon ground red pepper
¼ cup lime juice	Charred Corn Relish (recipe follows)
1 tablespoon chili powder	2 tablespoons chopped fresh cilantro
2 cloves garlic, minced	

PLACE chops in large resealable plastic food storage bag. Combine oil, lime juice, chili powder, garlic, cumin and ground red pepper in small bowl; mix well. Reserve 3 tablespoons mixture for Charred Corn Relish; cover and refrigerate. Pour remaining mixture over chops. Close bag securely, turning to coat. Marinate in refrigerator at least 8 hours or overnight, turning occasionally.

PREPARE grill for direct cooking. Prepare Charred Corn Relish.

DRAIN chops; discard marinade. Place chops on grid. Grill, covered, over medium heat 13 to 15 minutes for medium or until desired doneness, turning halfway through grilling time. Sprinkle with cilantro. Serve with Charred Corn Relish and corn bread, if desired.

Makes 4 servings

Charred Corn Relish

2 large *or* 3 small ears fresh corn, husked and silk removed	¼ cup chopped fresh cilantro
½ cup diced red bell pepper	3 tablespoons reserved lime juice mixture

PLACE corn on grid. Grill, covered, over medium heat 10 to 12 minutes or until charred, turning occasionally. Cool to room temperature. Cut kernels off each cob into large bowl and press cobs with knife to release remaining corn and liquid; discard cobs. Add bell pepper, cilantro and reserved lime juice mixture to corn; mix well. Let stand at room temperature while grilling chops.

Makes about 1½ cups

Maple-Glazed Turkey Breast

1 bone-in turkey breast
  (5 to 6 pounds)
¼ cup maple syrup
2 tablespoons margarine
  or butter, melted

1 tablespoon bourbon
  (optional)
2 teaspoons grated
  orange peel
Fresh bay leaves
  (optional)

PREPARE grill for indirect cooking.

PLACE turkey, bone side down, on roast rack or directly on grid, directly over drip pan. Grill, covered, over medium heat 55 minutes, adding 4 to 9 briquets to both sides of fire after 45 minutes to maintain medium heat.

COMBINE syrup, margarine, bourbon, if desired, and orange peel in small bowl; brush half of mixture over turkey. Continue to grill, covered, 10 minutes. Brush with remaining mixture; continue to grill, covered, 10 minutes or until internal temperature reaches 170°F when tested with meat thermometer inserted into thickest part of turkey, not touching bone.

TRANSFER turkey to carving board; cover with foil. Let stand 10 minutes before carving. Cut turkey into thin slices. Garnish with fresh bay leaves, if desired.   *Makes 6 to 8 servings*

Serving Suggestion: Serve with mashed sweet potatoes and sautéed squash with oranges.

Cook's Nook

For hickory-smoked flavor, cover
2 cups hickory chips with cold water; soak
20 minutes. Drain; sprinkle over coals just
before placing turkey on grid.

Honey and Mustard Glazed Chicken

....

1 whole chicken (4 to
   5 pounds)
1 tablespoon vegetable oil
¼ cup honey
2 tablespoons Dijon
   mustard
1 tablespoon soy sauce
½ teaspoon ground ginger

⅛ teaspoon black pepper
Fresh fruit and herbs
   (optional)

PREPARE grill for indirect cooking.

REMOVE giblets from chicken cavity; reserve for another use or discard. Rinse chicken with cold water; pat dry with paper towels. Pull skin over neck; secure with metal skewer. Tuck wings under back; tie legs together with wet string. Lightly brush chicken with oil.

COMBINE honey, mustard, soy sauce, ginger, pepper and salt in small bowl; set aside.

PLACE chicken, breast side up, on grid directly over drip pan. Grill, covered, over medium-high heat 1 hour 30 minutes or until internal temperature reaches 180°F when tested with meat thermometer inserted into thickest part of thigh, not touching bone. Brush with honey mixture every 10 minutes during last 30 minutes of cooking time.*

TRANSFER chicken to carving board; cover with foil. Let stand 15 minutes before carving. Garnish with fresh fruit and herbs, if desired. *Makes 4 to 5 servings*

*If using grill with heat on one side (rather than around drip pan), rotate chicken 180° after 45 minutes of cooking time.

Hot Wings with Creamy Cool Dipping Sauce

Creamy Cool Dipping
  Sauce (recipe follows)
¼ cup chopped onion
2 cloves garlic, minced
2 tablespoons olive oil
1½ cups prepared barbecue
  sauce

2 to 3 teaspoons hot
  pepper sauce
4 pounds chicken wings
  (about 16 to 20 wings)

PREPARE grill for direct cooking.

PREPARE Creamy Cool Dipping Sauce; cover and refrigerate until serving time.

PLACE onion, garlic and oil in medium microwavable bowl. Microwave at HIGH 1½ to 2 minutes or until onion is tender. Add barbecue sauce and pepper sauce; stir until blended. Set aside.

PLACE chicken on grid. Grill, covered, over medium-high heat 25 minutes or until chicken is no longer pink and juices run clear, turning after 15 minutes. Turn and brush with barbecue sauce mixture frequently during last 5 minutes of cooking time. Serve with Creamy Cool Dipping Sauce. Garnish as desired.

Makes 4 main-dish or 8 appetizer servings

Creamy Cool Dipping Sauce

⅔ cup mayonnaise
¼ cup Ranch-style salad
  dressing
3 ounces crumbled feta
  cheese

2 teaspoons finely chopped
  green onions
Green onion tops, sliced
  (optional)

COMBINE mayonnaise and salad dressing in small bowl. Stir in cheese and chopped onions; mix well. Sprinkle with green onion top slices, if desired.

Makes about 1¼ cups

Grilled Tuna and Succotash Salad

1 cup uncooked dried baby
  lima beans
$2/3$ cup vegetable oil
$1/4$ cup chopped fresh basil
3 tablespoons balsamic or
  red wine vinegar
2 tablespoons Dijon
  mustard
2 tablespoons lemon juice
$1/2$ teaspoon salt

$1/2$ teaspoon black pepper
4 tuna steaks (about
  6 ounces each)
1 cup frozen corn, thawed
2 large tomatoes, seeded
  and chopped
Fresh arugula or spinach
  leaves
Lemon slices and fresh
  dill sprigs (optional)

RINSE beans; place in large bowl. Cover beans with 4 inches of water; soak overnight at room temperature.

DRAIN beans and transfer to medium heavy saucepan; cover with water. Bring to a boil over high heat. Reduce heat to medium; simmer, covered, 40 to 45 minutes or until beans are tender. Drain; set aside.

COMBINE oil, basil, vinegar, mustard, lemon juice, salt and pepper in glass jar with tight-fitting lid. Cover. Shake well; set aside.

RINSE tuna; pat dry with paper towels. Place tuna in shallow glass dish. Pour $3/4$ cup oil mixture over tuna. Coat tuna in mixture; cover and marinate in refrigerator 30 minutes.

PREPARE grill for direct cooking. Transfer beans to large bowl. Add corn and tomatoes. Stir in remaining oil mixture. Cover; marinate at room temperature until ready to serve.

DRAIN tuna; discard marinade. Place tuna on grid. Grill over medium-high heat 6 to 8 minutes or until tuna flakes easily when tested with fork, turning halfway through grilling time.

ARRANGE tuna on arugula-lined plates. Spoon bean mixture over tuna. Garnish with lemon slices and dill, if desired.

Makes 4 servings

Peppered Beef Rib Roast

1½ tablespoons black
    peppercorns
1 boneless beef rib roast
    (2½ to 3 pounds), well
    trimmed
¼ cup Dijon mustard

2 cloves garlic, minced
Sour Cream Sauce
    (recipe follows)
Fresh rosemary and baby
    red onions (optional)

PREPARE grill for indirect cooking.

PLACE peppercorns in small resealable plastic food storage bag. Squeeze out excess air; close bag securely. Pound peppercorns using flat side of meat mallet or rolling pin until cracked. Set aside.

PAT roast dry with paper towels. Combine mustard and garlic in small bowl; spread over top and sides of roast. Sprinkle pepper over mustard mixture.

PLACE roast, pepper-side up, on grid directly over drip pan. Grill, covered, over medium heat 1 hour to 1 hour 10 minutes or until meat thermometer inserted into thickest part of roast registers 150°F for medium-rare or until desired doneness, adding 4 to 9 briquets to both sides of the fire after 45 minutes to maintain medium heat.

Meanwhile, **PREPARE** Sour Cream Sauce; cover and refrigerate.

TRANSFER roast to carving board; cover with foil. Let stand 5 to 10 minutes before carving. Serve with Sour Cream Sauce. Garnish with fresh rosemary and baby red onions, if desired.

Makes 6 to 8 servings

Sour Cream Sauce

¾ cup sour cream
2 tablespoons prepared
    horseradish
1 tablespoon balsamic
    vinegar

½ teaspoon sugar
Red onion slivers
    (optional)

COMBINE all ingredients except onion in small bowl; mix well. Garnish with red onion slivers, if desired. *Makes about 1 cup*